Nature's Children

BUFFALO

by Dan Doyle

Grolier Educational

FACTS IN BRIEF

Classification of the buffalo

Class:	*Mammalia* (mammals)
Order:	*Artiodactyla* (even-toed, hoofed mammals)
Family:	*Bovidae* (hollow-horned ruminants)
Genus:	*Bubalus*
Species:	*Arnee* (water buffalo); *Bubalus* (domestic buffalo)
Genus:	*Bison*
Species:	*Bison* (American buffalo)
Subspecies:	*Bison* (plains), *Athabascae* (wood)

World distribution. Water buffalo live in Nepal and Southeast Asia. Domestic buffalo are found primarily in India, Pakistan, and southeast Asia. Bison live throughout North America.

Habitat. Buffalo inhabit tropical and subtropical humid climates. Bison inhabit the plains and forests of colder climates.

Distinctive physical characteristics. Large animals weighing up to and over one ton; horned ruminants with shoulder humps and huge heads; color generally is some shade of brown or black.

Habits. Grazing and dozing.

Diet. Grass, herbs, and saplings.

Library of Congress Cataloging-in-Publication Data

Doyle, Dan, 1961-
  Buffalo / Dan Doyle.
    p.   cm. — (Nature's children)
  Includes index.
  Summary: Describes distinct physical characteristics, habitat,
diet, and behavior of buffaloes and bison; also indicates their
distribution throughout the world.
  ISBN 0-7172-9076-X (hardbound)
  1. Buffaloes—Juvenile literature. 2. Bison—Juvenile literature.
[1. Buffaloes. 2. Bison.] I. Title. II. Series.   97-5949
OL737.U53D69 1997   CIP
599.64'3—dc21   AC

This library reinforced edition was published in 1997 exclusively by:

 Grolier Educational

Sherman Turnpike, Danbury, Connecticut 06816

Set ISBN 0-7172-7661-9
Buffalo ISBN 0-7172-9076-X

Contents

Meet the Family   Page 6

The Water Buffalo   Page 8

Types of Water Buffalo   Page 11

Why Buffalo?   Page 12

Water Buffalo at Work   Page 14

Water Buffalo Products   Page 16

Milk and Cheese   Page 18

Yak It Up   Page 21

More Yakety Facts   Page 22

The Useful Yak   Page 24

Working Yaks   Page 26

A Tibetan Treasure   Page 28

Buffalo or Bison?   Page 29

The American Bison   Page 31

Buffalo in the Wild   Page 33

Buffalo: The Basis of a Life   Page 35

Senseless Slaughter   Page 37

Saving the American Bison   Page 38

A New Industry   Page 39

Buffalo Ranches   Page 41

The Return of the Buffalo   Page 42

The Wood Bison   Page 45

Saving the Wood Bison   Page 46

Words to Know   Page 47

Index   Page 48

When most of the world's people think of buffalo, they think of the water buffalo of Asia.

What comes to mind when you hear the word buffalo? Do you think of a large, long-haired, horned animal that roams the Western plains? If you live in North America, you probably do.

In other parts of the world, however, the word buffalo brings to mind a different creature. It, too, is large and has horns. But it usually has a smooth, shiny coat and is one of many farmers' most treasured domestic, or tame, animals.

In Asia, for example, farmers probably value the buffalo more than any other domestic animal. Buffalo are one of their main work animals and are used to do many different jobs. There farmers also raise buffalo for their milk and their meat.

Surprisingly, in North America the once-wild buffalo is also becoming a domesticated animal. Many herds are supervised and cared for by people. And people are even beginning to raise North American buffalo on ranches so that these animals can be used for meat and other products. This is part of a remarkable turnaround for an animal that once was almost extinct. And it is just part of the story of the world's domestic buffalo.

Meet the Family

Meet a family of animals called the Bovidae. This group of split-hooved creatures includes buffalo, yaks, and domesticated cattle. The family also includes bison, which is the correct name for the North American buffalo. Although these creatures, called bovids for short, vary in many ways, they are closely related and share several characteristics.

All bovids, for example, are ruminants, which makes them related to such animals as sheep, goats, and deer. Ruminants are cud-chewers. First they swallow their food. Then they bring it back up from one of the several compartments in their stomachs. The cud of food is then rechewed again and again until it is finally swallowed for the last time. In this way bovids get the most out of their food.

Bovids also have horns. Both male and female bovids have two hollow horns that stick out from high on their heads. Unlike the antlers of deer, however, bovids' horns do not branch, nor do they shed.

The North American bison (which is usually called a buffalo) is just one of the many members of the bovid family.

The Water Buffalo

Water buffalo, sometimes called Asian buffalo, are enormous animals. The biggest stand five to six feet (1.5 to 1.8 meters) at the shoulders and weigh up to 2,000 pounds (900 kilograms). Their crescent-shaped horns measure up to six feet (1.8 meters) across.

In the wild water buffalo are masters of the land. They are so fierce that angry buffalo have been known to attack elephants. Even the mighty rhinoceros and tiger treat the wild water buffalo with respect!

When not threatened, water buffalo are quiet, gentle animals. With few sweat glands, they spend much of their time in the water trying to beat the heat. By night they graze on water plants and, by day, doze and chew their cuds.

Unfortunately, buffalo are no match for humans. Over the years humans have hunted water buffalo for sport and profit. People have also brought them in contact with domestic cattle, from which water buffalo have caught deadly diseases. Once found in great numbers all over southern Asia, only a few scattered herds of water buffalo now exist in the wild.

The Asian water buffalo is a large and extremely useful animal.

Water buffalo can reach weights of up to 2,000 pounds (900 kilograms).

Types of Water Buffalo

Today the Asian water buffalo is mostly a domestic animal raised to help humans eat and work. Two separate types of water buffalo exist.

The first, the swamp type, is found in Southeast Asia, China, the Philippines, and Australia. Medium gray in color, swamp buffalo grow to anywhere from 1,000 to 1,600 pounds (450 to 720 kilograms). They can be recognized by the huge horns that stretch out from their bodies and by a V-shaped pair of stripes—like those that show a soldier's rank—on their chests. These creatures are raised to be work animals as well as to provide people with milk and meat.

The river buffalo is the second type. Although river buffalo vary a bit in color and size, most are dark or even black and weigh between 1,200 and 2,000 pounds (540 to 900 kilograms). Unlike the swamp buffalo, the river type has coiled horns that wrap in a circle. In most places it is used for meat and milk, although it is sometimes used as a work animal.

Why Buffalo?

Why do people raise buffalo? The answer is quite simple. To begin with, water buffalo are extremely hardy. In the wild they manage to get by in places in which even cattle would die of starvation. They also are amazingly healthy. Water buffalo rarely catch diseases.

There is another important reason for the popularity of water buffalo. These creatures are so gentle that almost anyone can handle them. Their care can often be left to the youngest child on a farm.

Beyond these reasons water buffalo live a long time. Even a hard-working animal has a life span of 30 to 35 years. And they help farmers by reproducing themselves frequently. Starting at the age of two, a female water buffalo will produce one calf a year for 16 years or more. And since these animals have few problems during pregnancy or birth, farmers can replace older animals—or even build a whole herd—quite easily. This makes water buffalo so valuable that an old Chinese saying goes, "If I die, you will weep, but if the water buffalo dies, you will starve."

The water buffalo is gentle among people, works hard, and costs little to feed.

Water Buffalo at Work

For hundreds of years the people of Asia have counted on water buffalo for labor. Water buffalo are strong enough to pull a plow, haul logs, or clear tree-covered land. With their large hooves they can keep a solid footing even in soft, muddy rice paddies.

Water buffalo also are used to power water pumps and simple machines such as mills and sugar cane presses. Even today water buffalo—not tractors—provide between a quarter and a third of all farm power in southern China and other Asian countries.

Water buffalo also are used to pull carts and wagons. These animals are experts at going cross-country, too, making their sure-footed way over hills and narrow, rock-covered trails as well as across rivers, streams, and muddy fields. Even in cities water buffalo still find a place, since many Asian cities still have roads that are not passable by trucks.

It's no wonder that it is hard to persuade Asian farmers to trade their water buffalo for tractors. After all, what tractor can reproduce itself or fuel itself on grass growing by the side of the road?

Few Asian farmers would give up their hard-working water buffalo.

Water Buffalo Products

The water buffalo is not just a work animal, of course. When its working days are over, most of these animals end up being used for other purposes. Some are even raised for those purposes from the start.

Water buffalo meat, for example, is highly prized in many parts of the world. According to just about everyone who has eaten the meat, it is quite delicious—even better, to most tastes, than beef. More important, it is more healthful, providing only half the harmful cholesterol of beef. This makes it just what many people are looking for—a lean, fairly healthful red meat.

Meat is not the only product that comes from the useful water buffalo. Leather is another one, and many countries have developed an industry producing the long-wearing but soft leather that comes from these animals' hides. There is even a demand for products made from the water buffalo's horns.

So little goes to waste when it comes to water buffalo that even the horns are used.

Milk and Cheese

Not all nonworking water buffalo end up as meat or leather. In fact, for many farmers water buffalo are too valuable as dairy producers to be used for meat or any other purpose.

Throughout Asia it is water buffalo milk—and not cow's milk—that people drink. In India, for example, 70% of the milk that people drink is buffalo milk. This same milk is also turned into butter and cooking oil. In some places buffalo milk is even turned into ice cream, yogurt, and evaporated milk.

In Europe, especially Italy, however, buffalo milk has a whole other use—cheese. Rich in milk solids and butterfat, buffalo milk makes excellent cheese. In fact, mozzarella cheese—which most North Americans know as the cheese on the top of pizza—was originally made of buffalo milk. Much of the mozzarella sold in supermarkets today actually comes from cow's milk. But to someone who loves traditional Italian food there is nothing that compares with the real thing, which is always made from the creamy white milk of the buffalo.

The gentle water buffalo produces some of the world's best cheese.

Because it doesn't have sweat glands, the Asian buffalo spends much of its time in the water trying to beat the heat.

Yak It Up

Another member of the bovid family is the yak. Originally from the mountains of central Asia, yaks have almost disappeared from the wild. In fact there are only about 1,000 wild yaks left in the world today. But there is no need to worry about the yak disappearing for good. More than 12 million yaks are kept for domestic use.

One of the most impressive features of any yak is its size. In the wild yaks grow to six feet (1.8 meters) tall and 1,100 to 1,200 pounds (499 to 544 kilograms) in weight. As the result of years and years of careful breeding, domestic yaks can grow even bigger than this.

Wild or domestic, these animals are well suited to their mountainous habitat. Their short legs and large, rounded feet make them sure-footed climbers. And their long, shaggy coats—which reach almost to the ground—help them withstand the cold winters. There is no need to worry about yaks in the summertime either. They shed most of their heavy coat in the spring.

Like other bovids yaks graze on grasses. Early morning and evening are their favorite times to eat. Wild yaks spend the rest of the day resting and chewing their cuds. Domestic yaks, of course, have other things to do.

More Yakety Facts

Given their size, you might expect yaks to be slow, clumsy creatures. But quite the contrary is true. In fact, they are graceful and can slide down slippery, ice-covered mountain slopes, swim against strong river currents, and make their way up steep, rock-covered hillsides.

Yaks are also noted for the sound they produce. Their popular nickname—the grunting ox—comes from their low, grunting sound.

To better survive in their habitat, yaks even have a special kind of blood. Wild yaks often live in areas more than 16,000 feet (4,870 meters) above sea level. There cold is not the only problem facing an animal. Up this high the air is so thin that some creatures have trouble getting enough oxygen into their bloodstreams. This gives them trouble breathing and even weakens them. (This is one reason why mountain climbers often have to be equipped with oxygen masks.)

Yaks have no such problem, however. Their especially thin blood takes in more oxygen than the blood of other mammals. As a result, yaks are able to survive—and even work—in all but the very highest altitudes.

Female water buffalo are attentive mothers, even though they often produce a calf each year for as long as 16 years!

The Useful Yak

For years yaks were hunted by the people who live in central Asia. In Tibet, Nepal, and other countries near the Himalayan Mountains yak meat always has been highly prized. With a flavor as delicate as beef, the meat is also low in fat and cholesterol. This makes yak meat, like other buffalo meat, a relatively healthful food.

Meat, of course, was not the only thing yak hunters brought back. The hides were especially valued for their leather, which was used to make everything from saddles and whips to tents and boots.

In spite of their size and ability to maneuver, yaks were fairly easy for hunters to kill. Once rifles were available, even the yak's ferocious charges could not stop the slaughter. As a result wild yaks are virtually gone today.

*The yak is an impressive animal that is put to good
use by the people of central Asia.*

Working Yaks

Domestic yaks serve their masters in many ways. One of the most important is as a means of transportation.

In Tibet, for example, yaks are often used to carry travelers. They also deliver the mail. And with their size, strength, and sure-footed walk, yaks make excellent pack animals. Able to bear extremely heavy loads, they can cover distances of 20 miles (32 kilometers) in a single day.

The fact that yaks are adapted to high altitudes makes them especially valuable. Expeditions climbing peaks such as Mount Everest rely on their trusty yaks to get heavy equipment and bulky supplies to the base camps from which they start their climbs up the mountains. No other animal— and certainly no motorized vehicles—could make it so safely over the steep rocky hillsides and passes at altitudes of 17,000 feet (5,200 meters) and more.

The yak's horns could be dangerous, but not dangerous enough to keep the wild yak from becoming almost extinct.

A Tibetan Treasure

For hundreds of years the people of Tibet have treasured their domestic yaks, which have an important place in the country's history and culture.

Tibetans, for example, rely on these amazing creatures to carry heavy loads, even over the most dangerous mountain passes. They also count on yaks for a steady supply of extremely rich milk. In fact, yaks provide so much milk that each female (called a dri) is usually milked three times each day. (Cows, in contrast, generally are milked only twice a day.) Yak milk is also turned into butter.

Beyond this Tibetans use the yak's soft underhair, spinning it into yarn and weaving it into cloth. The animal's coarse outer hair is put to use as well. Mats and tent coverings made from this coarser hair are especially strong. The hair is even used to make rope and harnesses.

Long ago Tibetans actually found a use for the yak's long tail, which has a thick tassel of hair at the end. For the people of those days these tails were such a symbol of power and status that high officials used them as decorations for their helmets!

Buffalo or Bison?

Did you know that the American buffalo is not really a buffalo at all? In truth this famous American creature, which is almost a symbol of life in the West, is a bison. The term buffalo actually applies only to two species of bovids, the Asian water buffalo and the African buffalo. The American bison, although it is closely related to these animals, is actually its own species.

If this is so, how did people start calling these creatures buffalo? French explorers and adventurers were probably the first Europeans to encounter this animal. They named these large, humpbacked, horned animals *les boeufs* (pronounced lay boofs), which means oxen.

Over the years people—especially those who did not speak French—turned the word boeuf into the English word buff, and in time the word buffalo. But the name buffalo has become so much a part of American culture that the American bison will most likely go on being called by its incorrect name forever. After all, can you imagine someone singing, "Oh, give me a home where the bison roam"?

Usually called a buffalo, the American bison the largest land animal on the continent.

The American Bison

Regardless of which name people use for it, the American bison is the largest of all North American land animals. Originally from Asia, it was one of the few bovid-type creatures to travel the prehistoric land bridge across the Bering Strait to North America.

There actually are two types of American bison, the plains bison and the wood bison. It is the plains bison, however, that most people think of when they hear the word buffalo. Brownish-black in color, these animals live on the Great Plains, the vast area that stretches across the central part of North America from the Mississippi River to the Rocky Mountains.

With its large head, shoulder hump, and black horns, the American bison is a striking figure. It is also a large one. Bulls (males) can reach weights of 2,000 to 3,000 pounds (900 to 1,350 kilograms) and can stand up to six feet (1.8 meters) tall at the shoulder.

When Europeans first came to the Great Plains, not much more than 300 years ago, between 30 and 70 million of these amazing animals lived there. Herds roamed freely from Canada to Mexico. Today, however, only about 120,000 remain. For the most part, they live in national parks or on game reserves or private ranches.

Buffalo in the Wild

Wild bison live in small bands made up family members and friends. These bands combine to form large, mixed herds of cows, calves, yearlings, and a few bulls.

The plains bison is amazingly well adapted to life in its habitat. To begin with, it is able to live in the temperature extremes that make life very hard for other creatures.

In late spring bison shed their coats in order to face the heat of summer. During this time they eat their fill of the fresh grass growing on the plains. In summer—the height of fly season— they wallow in marshes or dust bowls to rid themselves of flies. Then, as autumn approaches, bison grow thick coats to fight off the approaching winter temperatures, which can get astonishingly cold. In the winter the bison still manage to graze, swinging their large heads from side to side, pushing away the snow to get at the grass beneath it.

Other than disease and human hunters, one of the few dangers these creatures face is a stampede. Panicked by prairie fires, lightning, or tornadoes, they will run themselves almost to death, trampling nearly everything in their path—even each other.

Bison live in small bands of family members and friends that combine into large herds.

Buffalo: The Basis of a Life

Perhaps no culture in human history depended so much on a single animal as the plains Indians—the Pawnee, Cheyenne, Mandan, Sioux, and others—depended on the bison. For them the bison was a kind of general store, providing them almost everything they needed in order to survive. It is no wonder that before a bison hunt, these people honored the animal in dance and song.

From the bison these people of the plains got most of the meat they ate. Eaten fresh or dried for use later, it was the mainstay of their diet. Bison hides were turned into clothing, tepee coverings, shields, ropes, boats, and even coffins. The hair was used for ornaments and was braided into rope. Horns were made into drinking vessels, spoons, and ladles. Hooves were used to make glue, and fat provided hair grease.

Bison bones were turned into bows, arrowheads, scrapers, and toys for children. Tendons made thread, bowstrings, and webbing for snowshoes. The bison's ribs formed the runners of dogsleds, while the bladder and stomach were used to make containers. Even dried droppings, known to Europeans as buffalo chips, were used, making an excellent fuel for campfires.

A full-grown bison is an impressive sight.

This decorated buffalo skull dates back to the 1830s.

Senseless Slaughter

Before the arrival of Europeans the tribes of the Great Plains hunted bison on foot, using bows and arrows or making herds stampede over cliffs to their deaths.

In the 1500s, when Europeans brought horses to America, hunting became easier. On horseback hunters could pursue the bison, even choosing exactly which animals they would kill. The arrival of the gun made bison hunting easier still. Yet the number of bison killed by the plains Indians was small in comparison to the total population of these animals, which by 1851 was approximately 51 million.

The arrival of white settlers and the building of railroads quickly changed all this. By the late 1850s and early 1860s bison were being killed not by the thousands but by the millions. Some were killed for food, others for sport. When buffalo hide clothing and robes became fashionable, the animals were shot by professional hunters, and their carcasses were left on the ground to rot. Astonishingly, by 1865 only 15 million were left.

Things quickly got even worse for the bison. To clear land for settlers—and to deliberately eliminate the plains Indians' food supply—buffalo hunters slaughtered even more animals. By 1890 fewer than 1,000 plains bison were left.

Saving the American Bison

The story of the bison, however, has a happy ending. Remarkably, the American bison has recovered. In 1894 the U.S. Congress passed a law that made it illegal to shoot bison. A small herd of wild buffalo was maintained in the area that eventually became Yellowstone National Park. A few ranchers kept some small herds as well. Then, in 1905 President Theodore Roosevelt took steps that would, in time, lead to the bison's recovery.

A leader of the conservation movement in the United States, Roosevelt had lived in the West. Determined to save the West's most famous animal, Roosevelt helped found the American Bison Society. This group organized many efforts to bring the bison back from near-extinction.

It has taken many years and the efforts of thousands of people, but today there are more than 120,000 American bison. Some of these animals live freely in herds that roam state and national parks. There visitors can see, on a small scale, the sight of bison that thrilled the first European visitors to the West.

Most bison survive on ranches, where they are raised as domestic livestock.

A New Industry

During the years of senseless slaughter the buffalo was killed for sport, for fur, and even for the fertilizer that could be made from its bones. Today, however, it is the buffalo's meat that has led to its use as a domestic animal.

High in protein, with fewer calories and less fat and cholesterol than beef, bison meat is a thoroughly modern food. Lean and fast-cooking, it is both healthful and convenient. It has even won the endorsement of doctors and heart associations as an alternative to other red meats.

Buffalo meat, of course, is not something that is found in supermarkets everywhere. But it definitely is catching on. A restaurant near Denver, Colorado, for example, serves 50,000 dishes of buffalo meat each year—at an amazing price of $34.95 each! Another Colorado company turns buffalo meat into sausages, salami, and hot dogs.

Demand for buffalo meat definitely is growing, as are prices. Per pound, buffalo meat sells for anywhere from 50% to 60% more than beef. All this is a sign that the days in which buffalo were killed and left to rot on the plains are long gone.

Today, most bison live on ranches where they are raised as domestic animals.

Buffalo Ranches

With buffalo meat in such high demand, more and more ranches are raising the animals. In fact, by 1994 there were more than 1,000 buffalo ranches in the United States alone.

Ranchers are attracted to buffalo because of the high prices the meat can bring. They also appreciate the fact that buffalo (really bison, of course) are remarkably easy to raise. A full-grown buffalo eats 30 pounds (13.5 kilograms) of grass each day. Unlike cattle, which need additional—and expensive—feed in the winter, bison can manage to graze on snow-covered grass. Bison will even eat snow when they cannot find water—something else that cattle will not do.

Bison are also well adapted to life on the plains. They can even handle the very worst the winter can bring. This makes them an excellent choice for domestic ranchers and breeders.

Not everyone, of course, is convinced that bison will ever be a mainstay of either ranching or American diets. But there is little doubt that the interest in buffalo meat is helping to save this amazing animal.

The Return of the Buffalo

The return of the American bison has had an especially interesting effect. As ranchers have become more and more interested in raising these animals for profit, the people who once depended on the buffalo for their lives—the tribes of the West—are also turning to the buffalo.

In 1993, for example, an InterTribal Bison Co-operative was set up in Rapid City, North Dakota. Included in it are 29 tribes, all raising buffalo in herds that range in size from ten to 1,500.

One of the largest such operation is run by the Cheyenne River Sioux. Another is run by the Kalispel tribe in the northeastern part of Washington. Here, just as in the past, nearly every part of the bison is used. Meat, of course, is the main product. But the Kalispel operation, in particular, also sells everything from the hooves to the horns. Even the bones are made use of by local artists. Drawing on long traditions, tribal leaders are suggesting that the return of the buffalo—even as a domestic animal—can be an important part of life among Native Americans.

The return of the bison is one of the great success stories for animals.

The Wood Bison

For thousands of years the wood bison lived to the north of their plains bison cousins. Larger than plains bison, these creatures long inhabited the forests of western Canada. There, in northern Alberta, British Columbia, and the Northwest Territories, up to 170,000 of these creatures once made their home.

Like their cousins to the south, the wood bison seemed doomed to extinction. By 1957 their number had dwindled to a mere 200.

The government of Canada and the governments of several Canadian provinces, however, were determined to take action. In 1922 Wood Buffalo National Park— the largest national park in the world—was created. There, on land that straddles northern Alberta and the Northwest Territories, the government created a home for these creatures in an attempt to save them from disappearing forever.

By the 1990s the Canadian wood bison population had risen to 3,000. With several herds—in the Mackenzie Bison Sanctuary, in the Northwest Territories, at Elk Island National Park, and in other areas—hope grew that this threatened animal would survive.

Using their huge heads to knock away the snow, bison can graze even in the deep snows of the West.

Saving the Wood Bison

Saving the wood bison, however, has not been easy. In the early 1990s it was discovered that many of the animals at Wood Buffalo National Park were suffering from dangerous diseases, including tuberculosis. Since these diseases might spread to cattle—and threaten Canada's important cattle industry—there was concern.

One of the first suggestions for dealing with the problem was to eliminate the wood bison. Concerned citizens protested, and other remedies were tried. Luckily for the wood bison, these seem to be working.

Elsewhere herds are being kept in almost domestic conditions to protect the animals and build up the herd. One of the most interesting examples involves the Waterhen people, who have lived in this part of Canada for thousands of years.

In 1984, 34 wood bison were brought to the Waterhen lands in hopes of setting up a captive herd. In the years since, the herd and the people have done well together. Tourism and other industries—all based on the wood bison—have been started. It is hoped that as the herd increases, bison will help the Waterhen people as much as they did in the distant past.

Words to Know

Antler   A horn, usually on a deer, elk, or moose; antlers are grown and shed every year.

Bovids   Members of the bovidae animal family, including water buffalo, yaks, the American bison (known as buffalo), and oxen (cattle).

Butterfat   The fatty part of milk, from which butter is made.

Cholesterol   A fatty substance found in animal fats, known to have a harmful effect on health.

Cud   The mass of food brought up from the stomach of a ruminant; cud is chewed again and again before being swallowed and finally digested.

Mozzarella   A mild-flavored white cheese.

Paddies   Wet, marshy fields in which rice is grown.

Prairie   A large, mostly level grassy area with few trees.

Ruminants   Animals that eat grass and chew a cud; cattle, sheep, goats, buffalo (including bison), deer, camels, and giraffes are all ruminants.

Stampede   A rush of frightened animals.

Yearlings   Year-old animals

INDEX

Alberta, 45
American Bison Society, 38
antlers, 6
Asia, 5, 8, 14, 21, 24
Australia, 11

Bovidae, 6
bovids, 6, 21, 29, 31
British Columbia, 45

Canada, 45, 46
cheese, 18
Cheyenne, 35
Cheyenne River Sioux, 42
China, 11, 14
cholesterol, 16, 24, 39
Colorado, 39
cud, 6, 8, 21

deer, 6
Denver, Colorado, 39

elephants, 8
Elk Island National Park, 45

goats, 6
Great Plains, 31, 37

Himalayan Mountains, 24
horns, 6, 8, 11, 16, 31, 35

InterTribal Bison Cooperative, 42

Kalispel, 42

leather, 16, 18, 24

mail, 26
Mandan, 35
Mackenzie Bison Sanctuary, 45
meat, 5, 11, 16, 18, 24, 35, 39, 41, 42
milk, 5, 11, 18, 28
Mount Everest, 26

Nepal, 24
North America, 5, 31
Northwest Territories, 45

oxen, 22

Pawnee, 35
Philippines, 11
pizza, 18

ranches, 5, 41
roads, 14
Roosevelt, Theodore, 38
rhinoceros, 8
ruminants, 6

sheep, 6
Sioux, 35
Southeast Asia, 11
stampede, 33

Tibet, 24, 26, 28
tiger, 8
tractors, 14
trucks, 14

U.S. Congress, 38

Waterhen people, 46
Wood Buffalo National Park, 45, 46

Yellowstone National Park, 38
yogurt, 18